FORWARD/COMMENTARY

The National Institute of Standards and Technology (NIST) is a measurement standards laboratory, and a non-regulatory agency of the United States Department of Commerce. Its mission is to promote innovation and industrial competitiveness. Founded in 1901, as the National Bureau of Standards, NIST was formed with the mandate to provide standard weights and measures, and to serve as the national physical laboratory for the United States. With a world-class measurement and testing laboratory encompassing a wide range of areas of computer science, mathematics, statistics, and systems engineering, NIST's cybersecurity program supports its overall mission to promote U.S. innovation and industrial competitiveness by advancing measurement science, standards, and related technology through research and development in ways that enhance economic security and improve our quality of life.

The need for cybersecurity standards and best practices that address interoperability, usability and privacy has been shown to be critical for the nation. NIST's cybersecurity programs seek to enable greater development and application of practical, innovative security technologies and methodologies that enhance the country's ability to address current and future computer and information security challenges.

The cybersecurity publications produced by NIST cover a wide range of cybersecurity concepts that are carefully designed to work together to produce a holistic approach to cybersecurity primarily for government agencies and constitute the best practices used by industry. This holistic strategy to cybersecurity covers the gamut of security subjects from development of secure encryption standards for communication and storage of information while at rest to how best to recover from a cyber-attack.

Why buy a book you can download for free?   We print this so you don't have to.

Some are available only in electronic media. Some online docs are missing pages or barely legible.

We at 4th Watch Publishing are former government employees, so we know how government employees actually use the standards. When a new standard is released, an engineer prints it out, punches holes and puts it in a 3-ring binder. While this is not a big deal for a 5 or 10-page document, many NIST documents are over 100 pages and printing a large document is a time-consuming effort. So, an engineer that's paid $75 an hour is spending hours simply printing out the tools needed to do the job. That's time that could be better spent doing engineering. We publish these documents so engineers can focus on what they were hired to do – engineering. It's much more cost-effective to just order the latest version from Amazon.com

If there is a standard you would like published, let us know. Our web site is Cybah.webplus.net

NIST Special Publication 500-307

Cloud Computing Service Metrics Description

NIST Cloud Computing Program

This publication is available free of charge from:
https://doi.org/10.6028/NIST.SP.500-307

National Institute of
Standards and Technology
U.S. Department of Commerce

NIST Special Publication 500-307

Cloud Computing Service Metrics Descriptions

Frederic de Vaulx
Eric Simmon
Robert Bohn
NIST Cloud Computing Program
Advanced Networking Technologies Division
Information Technology Laboratory

This publication is available free of charge from:
https://doi.org/10.6028/NIST.SP.500-307

April 2018

U.S. Department of Commerce
Wilbur L. Ross, Jr., Secretary

National Institute of Standards and Technology
Walter Copan, NIST Director and Undersecretary of Commerce for Standards and Technology

Certain commercial entities, equipment, or materials may be identified in this
document in order to describe an experimental procedure or concept adequately.
Such identification is not intended to imply recommendation or endorsement by the
National Institute of Standards and Technology, nor is it intended to imply that the
entities, materials, or equipment are necessarily the best available for the purpose.

National Institute of Standards and Technology Special Publication 500-307
Natl. Inst. Stand. Technol. Spec. Publ. 500-307, 42 pages (April 2018)
CODEN: NSPUE2

This publication is available free of charge from: https://doi.org/10.6028/NIST.SP.500-307

This page is left intentionally blank

Reports on Computer Systems Technology

The Information Technology Laboratory (ITL) at the National Institute of Standards and Technology (NIST) promotes the U.S. economy and public welfare by providing technical leadership for the Nation's measurement and standards infrastructure. ITL develops tests, test methods, reference data, proof of concept implementations, and technical analyses to advance the development and productive use of information technology. ITL's responsibilities include the development of management, administrative, technical, and physical standards and guidelines for the cost-effective security and privacy of other than national security-related information in Federal information systems. This Special Publication 500-series reports on ITL's research, guidance, and outreach efforts in Information Technology and its collaborative activities with industry, government, and academic organizations.

National Institute of Standards and Technology Special Publication 500-307

Natl. Inst. Stand. Technol. Spec. Publ. 500-307, 42 pages (2018)

Acknowledgements

This document reflects the contributions and discussions by the members of the NIST Cloud Computing Reference Architecture and Taxonomy Working Group – Cloud Service Metrics Sub Group, led by Frederic de Vaulx of Prometheus Computing, LLC under contract with the U.S. Department of Commerce, National Institute of Standards and Technology, Information Technology Laboratory.

NIST SP 500-307 has been collaboratively authored by the NIST Cloud Service Metrics Sub Group.

NIST would like to acknowledge the specific contributions from the following contributors:

Jane Siegel (CMU)
Jacques Durand (Fujitsu)
John Calhoon (Microsoft)
Jeff Perdue (CMU)
Steve Woodward (Cloud Perspectives)
Alan Sill (TTU)
Ken E. Stavinoha (Solutions Architect. Cisco Systems)
Tom Rutt (Fujitsu)
Jenny Huang (AT&T)
Eric Roggenstroh (eGT for GSA)
Omar Fink (SAIC)
Steven J. McGee (SAW Concepts LLC)
Eric Simmon (NIST)
Scott Feuless (ISG/CSMIC)
Jim Watts (TSA)

Keyun Ruan (Chief Scientist, Espion Group, Ireland)
Jesus Luna (CSA)
William M. Fitzgerald (EMC Information Systems International, Ireland)
Kimberley Laris (Positive Assurance)
Massimiliano Rak (CerICT, Italy)
Neeraj Suri (Technical University of Darmstadt, Germany)
David Núñez (Universidad de Málaga, Spain)
Carmen Fernández-Gago (Universidad de Málaga, Spain)
Isaac Agudo (Universidad de Málaga, Spain)
Ron Kohl (R. J. Kohl & Assoc.)
Gary Rouse (GSA Contractor)
Jin seek Choi (Hanyang University, Korea)
Larry Lamers (VMWare)

Table of Contents

List of Figures

List of Tables

1 Executive Summary

With cloud computing in the mainstream, there is a preponderance of cloud-based services in the market and the choices for consumers increase daily. However, comparing the service offerings between cloud service providers is not a straightforward exercise. To be successful in procuring cloud services, one must have requirements that are clear, create service level agreements (SLAs) which reflect these requirements and be measureable in order to validate the delivery of these services along with their performance and remedies.

As part of the decision-making framework for moving to the cloud, having data on measurable capabilities, for example - quality of service, availability and reliability, give the cloud service customer the tools and opportunity to make informed choices and to gain an understanding of the service being delivered. National Institute of Standards and Technology's (NIST) definition of cloud computing [2] describes a "Measured Service" as being one of the five essential characteristics of the cloud computing model. To describe a "measured service", one needs to identify the cloud service properties that have to be measured and what their standards of measurement or metrics are.

A metric provides knowledge about a cloud property through both its definition (e.g., expression, unit, rules) and the values resulting from the measurement of the property. For instance, a customer response time metric can be used to estimate a specific response time property (i.e., response time from customer to customer) of a cloud email service search feature. It also provides the necessary information that is needed for to reproduce and verify measurements and measurement results.

In this context, the role of that metrics play is very important to support decision-making as well as:
- Selecting cloud services
- Defining and enforcing service agreements
- Monitoring cloud services
- Accounting and Auditing

Metrics for cloud computing services can be described using the model proposed in this document. The model represents the information needed to understand the targeted cloud property and which constraints should be applied during measurement. The Cloud Service Metric model (CSM) describes the higher-level concepts of the metric definitions for a specific cloud service property; service uptime is a prime example. Definitions for metrics contain parameters and rules to express a formal understanding the property of interest. The CSM model also contains elements to make the metrics concrete. Concrete metric definitions add specific values to rules and parameters that make the metric usable for a given scenario.

A scenario represents a particular use case in which metrics play a role. Stakeholders need to have a way to understand, assess, compare, combine and make decisions about cloud service properties. This means that for a given scenario (e.g., choosing a cloud service or setup a service agreement), a stakeholder needs to be able to get information on cloud service properties, which when measured will guide the stakeholder along the proper course of action. The scenario and cloud service property will determine the metric (standard of measurement) to be used.

2 Introduction

2.1 Audience

This document proposes a framework that identifies and characterizes the information and relationships needed to describe and measure properties of cloud services that are representative, accurate and reproducible. This information can be used in a variety of ways including, collection, comparison, gap analysis, and assessment or description of metrics at the technical or business levels. These metrics can connect information intended for decision-making, for the service agreements between provider and customer, for the runtime performance measurement and the underlying properties within the provider's system.

This document may be used as a source of information to better understand metrology within the context of cloud services, and as a framework to describe, collect and access information related to metrics. The measurement process and methodology necessary for performing the measurement of a given cloud property is not the focus of this document.

The targeted audience of this document includes but is not limited to:
- U.S. Government agencies
- Cloud service customers
- Cloud service auditors
- Cloud service providers

2.2 Background

Cloud computing shifted the use of compute resources from asset-based physical resources to service-based virtual resources. NIST in its definition of cloud computing [2] describes a "Measured Service" as being one of the five essential characteristics of the cloud computing model. Providing data on measurable capabilities (such as; quality of service, security features, availability and reliability) gives the cloud service customer the opportunity to make informed choices and to gain understanding of the state of the service being delivered. It also gives the cloud service provider the opportunity to present the properties of their cloud services to the cloud service customer.

However, cloud metrology is not necessarily well understood. Common terminologies (i.e. the definition of measurement, metric, and related concepts) or sets of measurement artifacts (i.e. unit of measurement, metric) often have several definitions, which makes it very difficult for the cloud service customer to compare services or rely on third party tools to monitor the health of the service. It also makes it difficult for the provider to show that the service is performing correctly or to allow its service to enter into a complex cloud service chain or federation.

Organizations, like U.S. agencies, need a way to consistently define sets of metrics on which they can rely, trust, and share. This has the net-effect of increasing the overall confidence in the results of measurements of selected cloud service properties. This effect also increases the support of the decision-making process during the different stages of the cloud service lifecycle.

It is critical to have the capacity to represent what needs to be measured, how the measurement results are used, and how they impact business and technical decisions.

Cloud metrology is vast and takes into account many different components, including:
- The definition of metric and its use
- The definition of measurement processes and methods
- The calibration of measurement tools
- The measurement operations
- The processing of measurement results and associated consequences

This document's primary focus is on the first item of the list and introduces an approach to define and represent the concepts and uses of measurement within the context of cloud services and their underlying components.

3   Definitions

Currently, the terminology of cloud service measurements is not well defined. Different stakeholders in the Information and Communication Technology (ICT) community use the same terms with slightly different (or sometimes contradicting or overlapping) meanings. This may be due to wide variety of ICT's technology domains (i.e. Software, Telecommunication, Manufacturing), each using its own language. It could also come from the lack of a common process to define new terminology. This leads to great confusion among cloud service providers, customers, carriers, and other cloud stakeholders.

The use of well-defined and understood terms within a given domain will enable the stakeholders to communicate more efficiently. It reduces the risk of the misinterpretation of information and facilitates the combination and comparison of information.

To bring clarity to the vocabulary of cloud service measurements, some of the core terms used in the document are defined below.

3.1   Cloud Service Metric

A metric applied to a cloud service property.

3.2   Cloud Service Property

A property specifically related to a cloud computing service.

3.3   Context

The circumstances that form the setting for an event, statement, or idea, in which the meaning of a metric can be fully understood and assessed.

3.4   Measurement

Set of operations having the object of creating a Measurement Result.

Note: Based on the definition of Measurement in ISO/IEC 15939:2007 [6]. Also used here to describe an actual instance of execution of these operations leading to the production of a Measurement Result instance.

3.5   Measurement Result

Value that expresses a qualitative or quantitative assessment of a property of an entity.

Note: Based on the definition of Measurement Result in ISO/IEC 15939:2007 [6]

Note: The term measure is **not** used in this document. Measure is defined with so many divergent definitions it is difficult to use. Section 9 "Definitions Survey" shows a sample of the definitions related to "measure".

3.6   Metric

A standard of measurement that describes the conditions and the rules for performing a measurement of a property and for understanding the results of a measurement.

Note: The metric describes what the result of the measurement means, but not how the measurement is performed.

Note: A metric is applied in practice within a given context that requires specific properties to be measured, at a given time(s) for a specific objective.

3.7   Property

A characteristic of a phenomenon, system or service to be measured. A property may be expressed qualitatively or quantitatively.

3.8   Unit of Measurement

Real scalar quantity, defined and adopted by convention, with which any other quantity of the same kind can be compared to express the ratio of the two quantities as a number [7].

Note: part of a Metric

4   The Role of Metrology in Cloud Services

Metrology – the science of measurement – is important for cloud computing not just for the measurement of properties of cloud services, but also to gain a common understanding of the properties themselves.

Physical properties can be measured using a standardized metrology process. Software properties measurement has some associated standards like functional size measurement methods [3][4][5] that are not exactly at the level of physical metrology.
Metrics are used to understand a particular measurement (or type of measurement) of a cloud service property and to understand the property itself by providing a standard for describing a measurement and measurement result.

Figure 1 shows the relationship between a property and a metric. Cloud services have properties that represent characteristics of the service. The understanding of these properties is very important to determine the service capabilities. One way to understand these properties is with metrics. The use of a metric through a measurement provides measurement results to estimate the property of an element. For instance, a customer response time metric can be used to estimate a specific response time property (i.e., response time from customer to customer) of a cloud email service search feature.

A metric provides knowledge about aspects of the property through its definition (e.g., expression, unit, rules). It also provides the necessary information for reproducibility and verification of measurements and measurement results.

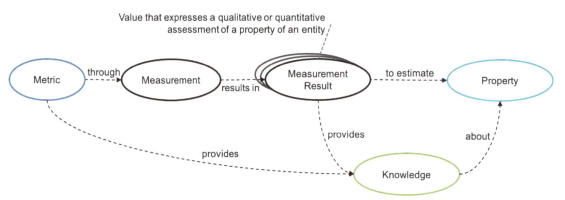

Figure 1 Metric and Property

In this manner, cloud metrics help providers communicate the properties of their cloud services that are measurable, help customers and providers agree on what will be provided, and allow cloud service features to be measured to ensure the agreement is met (and therefore the customers' requirements are met).

Cloud system can leverage metrics – standards for measurements – for many different purposes. For instance, metrics can be used at different layers of a cloud computing system (e.g., hardware layers, logic layers, governance layers or service layers). They can also be used at different stages of the cloud computing services life cycle (e.g., procurement, operation, audit and retirement).

4.1 The Cloud Service Trifecta

The use of metrics for cloud computing systems at the service interface can be broken down into three general areas, service selection, service agreement, and service verification. Metrics are essential, not just to understand each of these areas, but to connect these three distinct parts of the cloud procurement process. The three aspects of the trifecta are described below.

4.1.1 Metrics for Selecting Cloud Services

Metrics are essential at the stage of deciding what cloud offering should be best suited to meet the business and technical requirements. The customer of cloud services should be able to select and use metrics and their underlying measures to assess and decide which offering would be best. Solutions like the Service Measurement Index (SMI), [8] produced by the Cloud Services Measurement Initiative Consortium (CSMIC), could be used to determine which metrics are relevant to the selection of a particular cloud offering.

Figure 2 shows how metrics are used to understand the factors and properties necessary for distinguishing and deciding between two different cloud offerings. Such metrics may be used to provide data on actual cloud operations (e.g., performance, responsiveness, scalability, availability…) as produced by some independent auditing or monitoring of the provider when servicing its current customers. The use of these metrics may also result in an assessment on the readiness and ability of a cloud service provider to ensure some level of service quality prior to and independently from actual operations (e.g., various aspects of security, accessibility, customer support, financial flexibility).

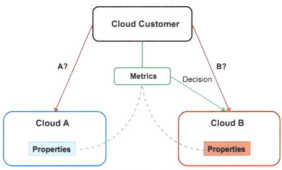

Figure 2 Cloud Service Selection

4.1.2 Metrics for Service Agreements (SAs)

A Service Agreement (SA) represents a binding agreement between the provider and customer of a cloud service. Among the elements that it contains are the description of the service, the rights and responsibilities of both the provider and the customer and terms definition. It also contains essential information related to the measurement of different aspects of the cloud service (e.g., its business level objectives or its performance level). The definition and usage of appropriate metrics with their underlying measures are essential components of the Service Level Agreement (SLA) and Service Level Objectives (SLO), which are constituents of the SA. The references [9] and [10] describe, in detail, the importance of and need for metrics in SLAs. At this point, the metrics are used to set the boundaries and margins of errors the provider of the service abides by and sets their limitations. For instance, these metrics could be used at runtime for service monitoring and balancing, or remediation (e.g., financial). Using a standardized set of metrics or metric templates in SAs makes it easier and quicker to define SLAs and SLOs, and to compare them with others.

Figure 3 illustrates the use of metrics to support an SLA document that defines the expectations of the two parties – cloud customer and cloud provider, allowing them to understand the characteristics of the specific service (cloud offering) being provided.

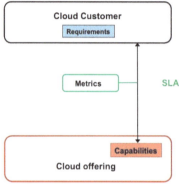

Figure 3 Cloud Service Agreement

4.1.3   Metrics for Service Measurement

Once the customer purchases a cloud service, it is necessary to ensure the service level objectives are being met. If they are not met, a pre-determined remedy needs to be initiated.
Figure 4 illustrates the service being delivered to the cloud customer from the cloud provider. In this case, metrics are used when monitoring the service level objectives defined in the service agreements.

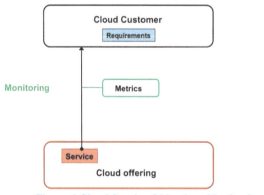

Figure 4 Cloud Service Objectives Monitoring

4.2   Other Metrics

Metrics can also be used internally within the cloud service itself. These metrics are more technical and used only by the cloud service provider to monitor and to understand the internal performance of their cloud system. References [11] and [12] discuss to specifications that show potential representations and usages of measurement concepts that can be used in cloud computing systems. Measurement results based on metrics for internal use may not be available to the cloud customer.

In addition, other parts of the cloud ecosystem can be influenced through the use of metrics like accounting, auditing and security. In the case of accounting, metrics are for instance linked to the amount of usage of a particular service. In the case of auditing, metrics are linked to the certification assessment of selected cloud service properties.

4.3 Scenario

Stakeholders need to have a way to understand, assess, compare, combine and make decisions about cloud service properties. This means that for a given instance, i.e. scenario (e.g. choosing a cloud service or setting up a service agreement), a stakeholder needs to be able to get information on cloud service properties, which when measured will aid the stakeholder in selecting the proper course of action. The scenario and cloud service property will determine the metric (standard of measurement) to be used. The measurement of the cloud service property through the metric will result in measurement results.

Figure 5 shows the scenario concept:
- The **Scenario** represents a particular use case (business process decision making, application monitoring, Service Level Agreements, etc.).
- The **Metric** describes the standard of measurement for a given cloud service property.
- The **Measurement Result** is data that results from making a measurement that follows a given metric.

More specifically, stakeholders (e.g. cloud customer or cloud provider) define the scenario for which the metric will be needed. The scenario represents:
- The expectations of an underlying business or operational process (e.g., SLA or Operation)
- How the metrics are used to assist in such a process
- What acceptable levels of the measured properties are

The scenario also includes the way the selected metrics are applied – what resource or service they support, under which conditions are their evaluation triggered and the frequency of the evaluation.

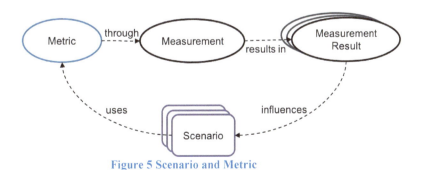

Figure 5 Scenario and Metric

9

In other words, a metric is a standard set of procedures and rules. In practice, the metric is applied within a given scenario that determines specific conditions, such as a specific resource(s) being measured, at a given time(s) for a specific objective.

Possible scenarios could be the application of an availability metric for a performance objective of 99% in an SLA scenario or the application of an accessibility metric for a usability objective of value "high" in a decision process scenario.

5   Cloud Service Metric Model

Understanding of the relationships between different data elements of cloud service metrology is very important in order to create meaningful and traceable metrics. This section introduces the Cloud Service Metric model (CSM), its general concept and a full element description of the foundation diagram that describes a Metric definition.

5.1   Cloud Service Metric Ecosystem

As explained in the earlier *Section 3,* a metric is a fundamental concept that provides information on how to understand a cloud service property being considered and how to estimate its value through measurements.

The information that comprises the metric ecosystem can be broken down into these specific aspects:

- The description and definition of a standard of measurement *(e.g. metric for customer response time) – CSM*
- The context related to using the CSM in a specific scenario. *(e.g. objectives and applicability conditions of the customer response time metric) – CSM Context*
- The use of the CSM to make measurements *(e.g. the measurement of response time property based on the customer response time metric) – CSM Measurement*
- The use of the CSM in a scenario *(e.g. the selection and use of the customer response time metric in an SLA) – CSM Scenario*

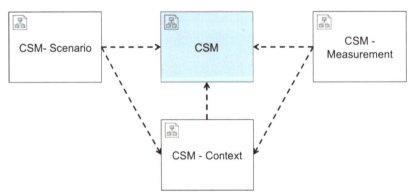

Figure 6 Cloud Service Metric Ecosystem Model

Figure 6 shows the breakdown of these different aspects and their relationships. The CSM box contains the description and definition of the standard of measurement. The CSM can be enhanced with information from the CSM Context; it contains elements that describe the environment a particular CSM is used in. The CSM Scenario relies on the CSM and the CSM Context and contains elements that describe use cases that rely on standards of measurement. The CSM Measurement relies on the CSM and the CSM Context and contains elements that are used during measurement operations.

In this document, the focus is on the CSM concept model (blue box) and not on the other surrounding concepts.

5.2 Model Criteria

The following are characteristics that were considered important when developing the CSM model.

5.2.1 Consistent Representation of Information

Information related to metrics should be represented in a consistent, repeatable way in order to efficiently organize it, share it and use it.

5.2.2 Explicit Relationships

Concepts like metrics should be represented in such a way that the relationships among them, if any, are explicit. This clarifies the effects these concepts have on one another and their importance.

5.2.3 Repository of Definitions

Metrics can be easily organized so they are reusable, searchable and derivable.

5.2.4 Comparability

The properties of the different concepts should allow its user to have enough information to efficiently compare them to find and understands either similarities or differences.

5.2.5 Flexibility and Adaptability

The model should be sufficiently flexible and adaptable to allow for easy integration with other metric models. These models could be complementary to the concept model (e.g. represent measurement methods and process).

5.2.6 Composability

The metrics should allow metrics definitions and instances to be reusable. Thus, one should be able to use one or more metrics to build a composite metric. This metric that is composed of underlying metrics builds upon the information they contain. This results in metrics that could possibly be composed of underlying metrics of different types of scales (e.g., qualitative and quantitative). This consideration will be discussed in *Section 8*.

5.3 Cloud Service Metric Diagram

This subsection formally describes the CSM diagram, its elements, what these elements are composed of and the way they are connected to each other.

Figure 7 introduces the CSM concept described as a Unified Markup Language (UML) class diagram [13]. The purpose of the CSM model is to capture the information needed to describe and understand a metric. The metric is used for gaining knowledge about and measuring cloud service properties.

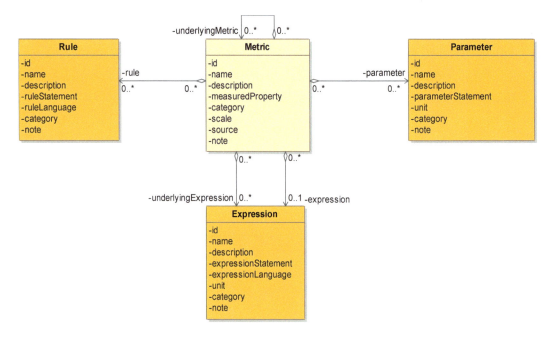

Figure 7 Cloud Service Metric (CSM)

5.4 Cloud Service Metric Element Definitions

The different elements of the CSM model are described below. In this section the use of the terms class, attribute and association and the model itself conform to the UML 2.0 specification. The classes are described in the following order; Metric, Parameter, Rule, Expression.

Within each class, the attributes are described, then the associations between the class and other classes. The attributes are described following the order of the diagram.

5.4.1 Metric Class

A Metric class defines the concrete standard of measurement for a specific cloud service property. The Metric class holds the basic information necessary to understand the measurement of a property to be measured. A metric becomes a way to understand what to measure and calculate with associated constraints

5.4.1.1 Metric Attributes

id

A unique identifier within a given organizational context. It uniquely identifies an instance. It is needed for references in expression and rule statements.
(e.g. RRT001)

name

A linguistic designation for the metric. It is not a unique identifier.
(e.g. Request Response Time)

description

Explanation that can be used by experts to gain a general understanding of the metric.
(e.g. "the response time of a cloud service to a single request, including request transit time, cloud services processing time, and response transit time")

measuredProperty

A categorization of the property a given metric provides a standard of measurement for. It can be used to organize metrics based on the measured property.
(e.g. service response time)

category

Classification of the metric which may be used to organize metrics, e.g. by different calculation methods or measurement approaches. It may also distinguish a class of metrics that does not have completely defined metric calculations or expressions.
(e.g. server request response time)

scale

Information on how the measurement value can be interpreted and what sort of operations can be performed on it. It is based on the theory of scales of measurement [14]. The scale also reflects whether a metric is qualitative or quantitative:

Qualitative – A metric that has either nominal or ordinal values. When nominal, the metric expresses a purely qualitative classification *(e.g. "good", "average", "bad")*. There is usually an expression (or formula) associated with each possible value, which is of qualitative nature. When ordinal, the metric expresses a ranked classification, where the degree of difference between rankings is undefined *(e.g. bronze, silver, gold)*. The **nominal** and **ordinal** scales are qualitative

Quantitative – A metric that has interval or ratio values, and can be expressed as multitudes or magnitudes. The **interval** scale allows for degree of difference between values while the ratio scale provides meaningful ratios between values.

Allowed values:
    Nominal
    Ordinal
    Interval

Ratio

source
The entity that produced the metric.

note
Any additional information related to the Metric. It provides information not included elsewhere in the metric that is helpful to understand or use the metric.

5.4.1.2 Metric Elements
expression
The main expression element representing the metric.

parameter
Parameters that are referenced in the expressions and rules of the metric.

rule
Rules that constrain aspects of the metric. Rules can constrain part of the metric expression or the entire metric. It doesn't contain the instances of rule elements of underlying metrics.

underlyingMetric
self-contained metrics that are used within the metric. Underlying metrics are usually referenced in the expression of the metric, but may be used within a rule or parameter.

underlyingExpression
Expression elements that are used in the expression of the metric. Underlying expressions can be used when an expression becomes too complex and big to be represented with only one expression.
(e.g. TimeDuration)

5.4.2 Rule Class

Used to provide constraints for the metric, expression, or parameter. For instance, an "AvailabilityDuringBusinessHour" metric element could be defined with a rule that limits the measurement period to a specific set of business hours. A constraint can be expressed in many different formats or languages (e.g. English, ISO 80000, SBVR)

5.4.2.1 Rule Attributes
id
A unique identifier within a given context (must be unique within the metric itself). It identifies a rule instance. It is needed for references in expressions, parameters, and other rules.
(e.g. RD001)

name
A linguistic designation for the rule. It is not a unique identifier.

description

Explanation of the rule that can be used by experts to gain a general understanding of the rule.

ruleStatement

Statement expressing the rule itself. It can reference other element instances including underlyingMetric, expression, or parameter if needed.

ruleLanguage

The language used in the ruleStatement.
(e.g. english)

category

A distinguisher which labels a class of rules used to organize rule elements by different condition methods or approaches. It may also distinguish a class of rules without completely defined rule expressions.

note

Additional information related to the rule. It provides information not included elsewhere in the rule.

5.4.3   Parameter Class

A parameter element is a reference or value that is passed to an expression or rule statement. A parameter's value is determined before the metric is used in a measurement. A parameter element can be referenced by more than one metric expression or rule statement.

5.4.3.1   Parameter Attributes
id

A unique identifier within a given context (must be unique within the metric itself). It identifies a paramter instance. It is needed for references in expression and rule statements.
(e.g. PD001)

name

A linguistic designation for the parameter. It is not a unique identifier.

description

Text explanation that can be used by experts to gain a general understanding of the parameter.

parameterStatement

The statement or value of the parameter

unit

The unit of the parameter statement if needed

category

A distinguisher which labels a class of parameters used to organize parameter elements by different condition methods or approaches. It may also distinguish a class of parameters without completely defined parameter expressions.

note

Additional information related to the parameter. It provides information not included elsewhere in the parameter.

5.4.4 Expression Class

The structure of a metric is expressed by the expression element. An expression may reference; underlying metrics, parameters, rules and underlying expressions. In a metric expression, a measurable element is expressed with an underlying metric, a calculated or complex element can be expressed with an underlying expression. An expression element can be referenced in more than one metric expression.

5.4.4.1 Expression Attributes
id

A unique identifier within a given context (must be unique within the metric itself). It identifies a expression instance. It is needed for references in expression statements.
(e.g. EXP001)

name

A linguistic designation for the expression. It is not a unique identifier.

description

Text explanation that can be used by experts to gain a general understanding of the expression.

expressionStatement

Statement representing the function used to assemble the underlying metrics, parameters and underlying expressions that compose the metric. Rules can also be part of the expression to constrain parts of it. In its most simple form, the expression is a literal, but it can also be a more formal expression language.
(e.g. expression = Sum(ResponseTime)/n where "ResponseTime" represents an underlying metric and "n" is a parameter element)

expressionLanguage

The language used in the expressionStatement
(e.g. ISO80000)

unit

The unit of the output of the expression. Note, the unit of the first expression (i.e. the metric primary expression) is the same as the metric output unit. *(e.g. second)*

Also note, not every metric is associated with a scalar unit of measurement. For instance, metrics whose scale is nominal or ordinal (i.e. qualitative metrics) could be associated to a list of classifiers (e.g. low, medium, high for data sensitivity) or a more complex construct.

category

A classification of expressions used to organize expression elements by different condition methods or approaches. It may also distinguish a class of expressions without completely defined expression statements.

note

Additional information related to the expression. It provides information not included elsewhere in the expression.

6 How to Use the CSM Model

The CSM model defines the fundamental elements needed to describe standards of measurement (i.e. metrics). The concepts and attributes in the CSM model allow one to use it in different ways. Figure 8 illustrates a couple different scenarios of use of the model (the scenarios will be more explained in the next section)

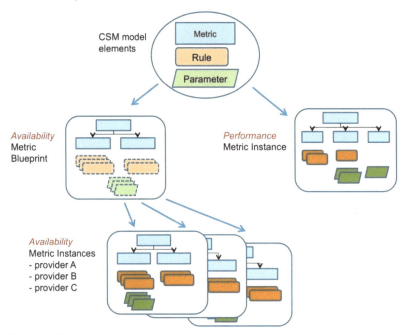

Figure 8 CSM Model Scenario Examples

At the top of the diagram there are the elements of the model. On the left path these elements are used to first create a blueprint of the metric for availability. This blueprint is then used to create concrete instances of the availability metric for different providers. On the right path these elements can also directly be used to describe an existing instance of a performance metric.

6.1 CSM Model Use Cases

The model supports several use cases including the use cases described in this section.

6.1.1 Express a Description for an Existing Metric (UC1)

UC1 – To express existing metric description in plain English using the base concepts – i.e. metric, expression, rule, parameter – (e.g. starting from an existing cloud SLA metric).

- **Rationale**: often the metric(s) information is scattered over a document text (measurement rules, exceptions, underlying quantities and metrics, etc.) and is mixed with related info that is not part of the metric definition per say (performance objectives, remediation measures and penalties, etc.). Distinguishing metric definition in a specific structure has proven to be of great value to understand the metric in use.

6.1.2 Create a Description for New Metric (UC2)

UC2 – To develop metric descriptions from scratch (e.g. elasticity metric)

- **Rationale**: Engineers as well as SLA writers and auditors need some framework to describe and design metrics. A metric model or structure helps define a sharable representation, and also detect missing components. The metric can be defined using existing components. This is important to ensure new metrics are created using a structure that can match existing metrics, so they can be used or exchanged harmoniously. This use case provides the template and process for creating a metric.

6.1.3 Formalize a Metric Description (UC3)

UC3 – To formalize metric expressions and rule statements from plain English to formal languages thus creating a path to metric description maturation (e.g. go from CSLA metric English expression language to ISO80000 expression language).

- **Rationale**: it is convenient to use the same overall metric structure, when translating a plain text description of a metric into a more formal representation closer to its execution. These are two steps (plain text, formal) in the design process of a metric. Converting a metrics expression from plain language to formal language is necessary to dissect a metric into its variable components in order to relate the metric to the CSM so that similar metrics can be minimized to reduce duplication.

6.1.4 Generalize a Metric Description (UC4)

UC4 – To generalize metric description and comparison based on a category (e.g. generic availability metric) in order to develop a blueprint.

- **Rationale**: Defining the foundational elements of the metric gives users a reusable starting point for the creation of new metrics and helps identify when metrics are truly different or just variations on the same general blueprint. In many cases it is desirable to share the same metric foundation if not the same metric. For example, there are many variants of a "service availability percentage" metric across providers. But can we say these providers share a similar general meaning of what is measured (availability percentage)? And how can we identify this common base? Extracting a metric blueprint from a set of metrics is a way to identify this base. A "service availability metric blueprint" captures what is common to several flavors of "service availability" while making the differences easier to spot across providers (often important "details", e.g. exception rules, etc.). This blueprint in turn makes it easier for a Cloud user to compare these metric variants. A metric description blueprint can be seen as partially defined metric.

6.1.5 Reuse Metrics Elements Across Metrics (UC5)

UC5 – To define standalone metric elements like rules, parameters or expressions that can be reused in different descriptions.

- **Rationale**: Reuse of certain standard elements comprising cloud service metrics can help to ensure consistency across metrics and ease the process of creating them. A catalog of reusable elements could include such things as standard expressions for unit conversion (time, temperature, etc.) and standard parameters for the number of days in a month, which one would expect to be the same across many or all metrics.

6.2 Matrix

As explained in the previous section the CSM allows one to describe a metric following different scenarios. This increases the flexibility of the model, but it is therefore possible that not all fields are necessary for all the scenarios. Table 1 lists all the elements and fields of the CSM model and suggests what field should be present given a use case described in the previous section.

- 'R' means that the field must be present.
- 'X' means that the field is not required but suggested.
- '-' means that the field is optional for a given scenario.

Table 1 CSM Model Elements and Attributes Matrix

Concept/Property	UC1/UC2/UC3	UC4	UC5
Metric			
id	R	R	R
name	-	-	-
description	-	-	-
measuredProperty	-	R	X
category	-	R	X
note	-	-	-
scale	X	X	X
source	-	-	-
expression	R	R	R
parameter	-	-	-
rule	-	-	-
underlyingMetric	-	-	-
underlyingExpression	-	-	-
Expression			
id	R	R	R
name	X	X	X
description	-	-	-
expressionStatement	R	R	R
expressionLanguage	R	R	R
unit	R	X	X
category	-	R	X
note	-	-	-
Parameter			
id	R	R	R
name	-	-	-
description	-	-	-
parameterStatement	X	X	X
unit	R	X	X
category	-	R	X
note	-	-	-
Rule			
id	R	R	R
name	-	-	-
description	-	-	-

ruleStatement	R	X	X
ruleLanguage	R	X	X
category	-	R	X
note	-	-	-

7 Measurement Uncertainty

In metrology, the result of a measurement is not meaningful if a statement of the uncertainty of the measurement is not specified. This statement allows users to assess the quality of the measurement results and to build confidence to compare results and use them within the range of the measurement uncertainty.

The International Vocabulary of Metrology (VIM) [7] defines measurement uncertainty as

A non-negative parameter characterizing the dispersion of the quantity values being attributed to a measurand, based on the information used

NOTE 1 Measurement uncertainty includes components arising from systematic effects, such as components associated with corrections and the assigned quantity values of measurement standards, as well as the definitional uncertainty. Sometimes estimated systematic effects are not corrected for but, instead, associated measurement uncertainty components are incorporated.

NOTE 2 The parameter may be, for example, a standard deviation called standard measurement uncertainty (or a specified multiple of it), or the half-width of an interval, having a stated coverage probability.

NOTE 3 Measurement uncertainty comprises, in general, many components. Some of these may be evaluated by Type A evaluation of measurement uncertainty from the statistical distribution of the quantity values from series of measurements and can be characterized by standard deviations. The other components, which may be evaluated by Type B evaluation of measurement uncertainty, can also be characterized by standard deviations, evaluated from probability density functions based on experience or other information.

NOTE 4 In general, for a given set of information, it is understood that the measurement uncertainty is associated with a stated quantity value attributed to the measurand. A modification of this value results in a modification of the associated uncertainty.

In the context of cloud services, it is critical that the consumer of a measured resource be confident about the measurements operated on that resource. These measurements will feed metrics that could be used against thresholds to determine the range the acceptable results and trigger possible consequences.

The current CSM model starts addressing this aspect of metrology with an attribute "uncertainty" that is contained in the CSM Measurement model.

8 Other Considerations

8.1 Metrics used for Property Composition

A key aspect of the CSM model is its extensibility, which permits metric definitions to be composed from other metric definitions. This is an effort to limit the duplication of information without too much of an increase on complexity. CSM allows qualitative or quantitative metrics to be defined and composed. This can affect the estimation – measurement results – of a particular property in several ways like its uncertainties.

8.2 Calibration & Measurement

Once new metrics have been defined for cloud service properties that can be reusable and comparable, the next step could be the calibration of the measurement systems used for measurement of cloud service properties against established measurement standards. This will enable a better alignment of the understanding and comparison of the properties that compose different cloud service offerings.

9 Conclusion

Metrics are a critical aspect of the selection, operation and use of cloud services. Metrics allow stakeholders to gain a better understanding of cloud service properties through consistent, reproducible and repeatable measurements. Metrics can be used for a wide range of objectives from decision making to operation. For instance, key performance indicator metrics can be used to measure specific achievements whereas benchmark metrics can be used as reference to compare features against one another.

Metrics need to be well defined and understood so that the different cloud computing stakeholders can use them with confidence. The Cloud Service Metric (CSM) model proposed in this document is one approach to addressing these challenges. The CSM defines a set of concepts and relationships to define what a metric is, what it is composed of, and what constrains it.

The CSM model can be leveraged for for use in several scenarios including; describing existing metrics, describing new metrics, formalizing metrics, generalizing metrics and creating blueprint of metrics

The CSM model can be extended and integrated into other models that address other aspects of the metric ecosystem like the context of a metric, the measurement and measurement results based on a metric or the scenarios that make use of metrics. These other aspects will be explored in future work.

Annex A - Cloud Service Metric Description Example

A.1 Provider Daily Mean Response Time Metric

Scenario

In this scenario a cloud service customer (CSC) is purchasing a SaaS cloud computing service and has a cloud service level agreement CSLA with the cloud service provider (CSP). One of the service level objectives (SLOs) contained in the CSLA is monitor that the daily mean valid request response time property stays within the agreed terms. This SLO is based on a CSP daily mean response time metric as indicated in the assumptions below.

This example demonstrates the use of the CSM model proposed in *Section 5.3* by creating instances of the concepts in a graph and table format. This example applies to the CSM use case 2 and 3 (UC2, UC3) laid out in *Section 6.1*. A new cloud service metric is described from the scenario requirements and formalized.

The CSM conceptual model gives the flexibility to its user to describe metric in a few different ways with the use of underlying metrics, underlying expressions and rules. In this example, every measurable element is described using underlying metrics.

Note that this scenario focuses on one specific metric of response time and that it is probably not the only metric of response time. For the sake of clarity and to avoid confusion the study of other response time metrics in this example is out of scope.

The scenario is using the following assumptions:
- The response time measurements are triggered for every valid request
- A request is considered valid if
  - It is of the correct service type
  - It conforms to the cloud service API
- The response time measurements are made over a measurement period of 1 day
- We are measuring the response time of a SaaS cloud computing service
- The CSP is making the response time measurement.
  - The measurement starts when the end of the request message is received at the service interface
  - The measurement stops when the beginning of the response message is sent from the service interface. Note that by stopping the measurement at the beginning of the message and not at the end, this metric doesn't take into account the size of the response.

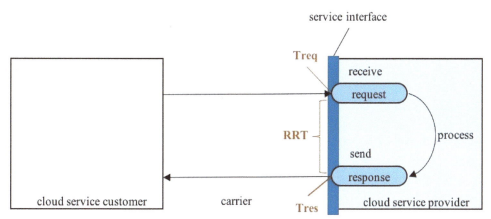

Figure 9 Diagram of the example scenario

Figure 9 depicts the scenario chosen for this example. A cloud service customer sends a request message to a cloud service provider which processes it and sends back a response. The bold blue vertical line on the CSP side represents the cloud service interface (service boundary) that separates the cloud service provider from the outside. **Treq** and **Tres** are the time of the request and the time of the response respectively. The Request Response Time (**RRT**) is a time duration and will be calculated by subtracting the 2 times. The Provider Daily Mean Valid Request Response Time (**DaMeVRRT**) will be calculated by taking the mean of the RRTs for all valid requests over 1 day. A valid request is determined based on the assumptions described above.

In this scenario, each request-response pair is associated with a correlation id (i.e. A, B, C, D and E), ReqA is of the wrong service type. ReqB, C, D and E are of the correct service type. In addition, ReqD has its corresponding response ResD outside the measurement period and ReqE doesn't have a corresponding response. Given the rules in table 2 A, D and E will fail and not be taken into consideration during measurement.

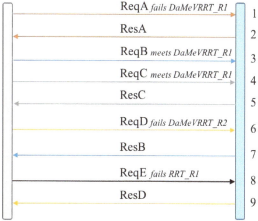

Figure 9 Request-response sequences

Figure 10 shows sequences of request – response messages used in the scenario. The number on the right side of each message represents the number index of the message but also the measured time for either TReq or TRes. For instance, ReqB has TReq = 3ms and ResB has TRes = 7ms.

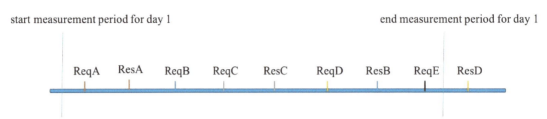

Figure 10 Request-response timeline

Figure 11 shows the request-response sequences in a timeline. It also adds the beginning and end of the measurement period. This shows that ResD for instance is out of the measurement period and thus might be affected by the metric rules.

Table 2 is a summary of all the rules constraining the metrics described in this scenario. Each row represents the set of rules that apply to a metric described in this scenario. For instance, the first row contains the rules for the DaMeVVRT metric.

Table 2 Scenario rules

Rules
DaMeVRRT_R1: RRT Req must be valid, Req is valid if It is of the correct service type and it conforms to the cloud service API **DaMeVRRT_R2**: RRT Treq and Tres must be within measurement period **MeasPer_R**: Measurement period MeasPe_P is daily
RRT_R1: Request-response must be complete; request-response is complete if a request has an associated response **RRT_R2**: Request and response are linked by the same CoId_P
Tres_R1: Time is measured for a response **Tres_R2**: Response is associated to a CoId_P
Treq_R1: Time is measured for a request **Treq_R2**: Request is associated to a CoId_P **ReqCoId_R**: CoId_P is assigned when a request is received

Table 3 shows the DaMeVRRT metric used in a measurement for this scenario. Each column represents a metric and the measurement results taken for this scenario.

Using the data from figure 9 and 10 and the rules from table 2, the time for each request and response has been measured. E failed rule RRT_R1 so RRTE is not calculated. The rest of the RRTs are measured. A failed rule DaMeVRRT_R1 because ReqA is of the wrong service type so RRTA won't be taken into consideration. D failed rule DaMeVRRT_R2 because ResD came after the end of the measurement period, so RRTD won't be taken into consideration. DaMeVRRT is then measured with RRTB and RRTC.

Table 3 Scenario through numbers

TReq (ms)	TRes (ms)	RRT (ms)	DaMeVRRT (ms)
TReq	TRes	RRT = TRes - TReq	DaMeVRRT = Sum(RRT_i)/|RRT|
TReqA = 1		RRTA = 2-1 = 1	
	TResA = 2		
TReqB = 3		RRTB = 7-3 = 4	
	TResB = 7		
TReqC = 4		RRTC = 5-4 = 1	$DaMeVRRT_{day1}$ = (4+1)/2 = 2.5 VRRT = {RRTB,RRTC}
	TResC = 5		
TReqD = 6		RRTD = 9-6 = 3	
	TResD = 9		
TReqE = 8		RRTE = N/A	

Metric Description Instance

This section presents the DaMeVRRT metric description along with its rules, parameters and underlying metrics. Two formats are used below to describe the metrics, a graph format and a table format. The graph format shows how the different metrics, rules and parameters are connected together. The table format shows the detailed description of the different elements represented in the graph format. These two formats are not the only ways to represent the metric description. XML, YAML, JSON formats can also be used in order to get computable versions of the description.

The graph in Figure 12 a high-level view of the metric and how it relates to its underlying metrics and the other elements like expressions, rules and parameters. It shows how each metric is "encapsulated" – i.e. it can stand on its own and it contains the relationships with the expressions, rules and parameters necessary to be understood. In the graph below, blue circles represent metrics, grey rectangles represent expressions, yellow rectangles represent rules and orange rectangle represent parameters. The directed arrows represent the relationships between metrics, expressions, rules and parameters. Some directed arrows also have a "n" or "1" to one end of the link. This represents the multiplicity of the relationship. The "n" multiplicity between DaMeVRRT and RRT means that the DaMeVRRT metric will use multiple RRT metric measurement results for the measurement of one DaMeVRRT metric. The "1" multiplicity between RRT and TReq or TRes means that RRT will only use one TReq measurement result for the measurement of one RRT metric.

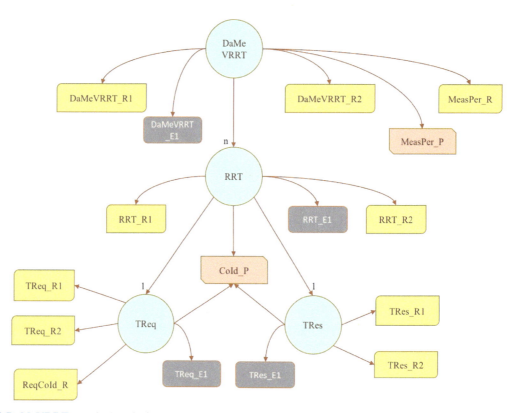

Figure 12 DaMeVRRT metric description graph

The tables below represent the description of the different metrics, rules, parameters and expressions used in this scenario. The blue tables are metric descriptions. The yellow tables are rule descriptions and the orange tables are parameter descriptions. Expressions are lumped in with the metric description.

Metric (Daily Mean Valid Request Response Time, DaMeVRRT)	
measuredProperty	daily mean valid request response time
category	mean response time
scale	ratio
parameter	MeasPer_P
rule	DaMeVRRT_R1 DaMeVRRT_R2 MeasPer_R
underlyingMetric	RRT
underlyingExpression	DaMeVRRT_E1

expression (DaMeVRRT_E1)		
id	expressionStatement (expressionLanguage)	unit
DaMeVRRT_E1		ms

		$$\frac{\sum_{i=1}^{i=|RRT|} RRTi}{|RRT|}$$ (ISO 80000)	
	note		

Rule (DaMeVRRT_R1)	
ruleStatement	RRT request must be valid, a request is valid if: • It is of the correct service type • It conforms to the cloud service API
ruleLanguage	English
category	valid request constraint

Rule (DaMeVRRT_R2)	
ruleStatement	RRT Treq and Tres must be within measurement period MeasPer_P
ruleLanguage	English
category	measurement window constraint

Rule (MeasPer_R)	
ruleStatement	Measurement period MeasPer_P is daily
ruleLanguage	English
category	measurement period constraint

Parameter (Measurement Period, MeasPer_P)	
parameterStatement	
unit	{hh:mm:ss, hh:mm:ss}
category	Measurement period
note	Interval for purpose of measurement

Metric (Request Response Time, RRT)	
measuredProperty	request response time
category	response time
scale	ratio
parameter	CoId_P
rule	RRT_R1 RRT_R2
underlyingMetric	TReq TRes
underlyingExpression	RRT_E1
expression (RRT_E1)	
id	expressionStatement (expressionLanguage)	unit

RRT_E1	$$TRes - TReq$$ (ISO 80000)	ms
	note	

Rule (RRT_R1)	
ruleStatement	Request-response must be complete; a request-response is complete if a request has an associated response
ruleLanguage	English
category	request-response constraint

Rule (RRT_R2)	
ruleStatement	Request and response are linked by the same CoId_P
ruleLanguage	English
category	request-response relationship constraint

Metric (Time of Request, **TReq**)		
measuredProperty	time of request	
category	time duration	
scale	ratio	
parameter	CoId_P	
rule	TReq_R1 TReq_R2 ReqCoId_R	
underlyingExpression	TReq_E1	
expression (TReq_E1)		
id	**expression (expressionLanguage)**	**unit**
TReq_E1	time as defined in ISO 80000 series (English)	ms
	note	

Rule (TReq_R1)	
ruleStatement	Time is measured for a request
ruleLanguage	English
category	measurement constraint

Rule (TReq_R2)	
ruleStatement	request is associated to a CoId_P

ruleLanguage	English
category	correlation constraint

Rule (ReqCoId_R)	
ruleStatement	CoId_P is assigned when a request is received
ruleLanguage	English
category	correlation constraint

Metric (Time of Response, **TRes**)		
measuredProperty	time of response	
category	time duration	
scale	ratio	
parameter	CoId_P	
rule	TRes_R1 TRes_R2	
underlyingExpression	TRes_E1	
expression (TRes_E1)		
id	**expression (expressionLanguage)**	**unit**
TRes_E1	time as defined in ISO 80000 series (English)	ms
	note	

Rule (TRes_R1)	
ruleStatement	Time is measured for a response
ruleLanguage	English
category	measurement constraint

Rule (TRes_R2)	
ruleStatement	Response is associated to a CoId_P
ruleLanguage	English
category	correlation constraint

Parameter (Correlation Id, **CoId_P**)	
parameterStatement	
unit	-
category	correlation identifier
note	

Annex B - Definitions Sample

Table 4 presents a sample collection of measurement terms and definitions coming from different domains including, information technology, software, software engineering and physical. The terms that were sampled are measure, metric, key performance indicator, benchmark, measurement and measurement unit. As result, the table shows that across and among domains there are many different definitions for the same term. Most of these definitions tend to have the same concepts in their descriptions however a few mix the terms and definitions. For instance the OMG SIMM document defines measure as "a method assigning comparable numerical or symbolic values to entities in order to characterize an attribute of the entities" and measurement as "a numerical or symbolic value assigned to an entity by a measure" and other documents used the same definitions but inverted the terms so in the case of the ISO/IEC 15939 document measurement is defined as "Set of operations having the object of determining a value of a measure" and measure as "variable to which a value is assigned as the result of measurement".

Table 4 A sample of measurement related terms and definition in the IT space

Term	Source	Title	Organization	Category	Description
				measure	
base measure	ISO/IEC 15939	Systems and software engineering - Measurement process	ISO/IEC	software engineering	measure defined in terms of an attribute and the method for quantifying it
measure	ISO/IEC 15939	Systems and software engineering - Measurement process	ISO/IEC	software engineering	variable to which a value is assigned as the result of measurement
measure	ISO/IEC 15939	Systems and software engineering - Measurement process	ISO/IEC	software engineering	make a measurement
measure	NIST SP 500-209	Software Error Analysis	NIST	software engineering	The numerical value obtained by either direct or indirect measurement; may also be the input, output, or value of a metric.
measure	IEEE 1061	IEEE Standard for a Software Quality Metrics Methodology	IEEE	software engineering	(A) a way to ascertain or appraise value by comparing it to norm. (B) to apply a metric
measure	SAMATE	SAMATE Project	NIST	software assurance	we use measure for more concrete or objective attributes
measure	SMM	Structured Metrics Metamodel (SMM)	OMG	software engineering	a method assigning comparable numerical or symbolic values to entities in order to characterize an attribute of the entities
quantity	JCGM 200:2012	International vocabulary of metrology - Basic and general concepts and associated terms	BIPM	metrology	property of a phenomenon, body, or substance, where the property has a magnitude that can be expressed as a number and a reference
				metric	
base metric	DSP1053_1.0.1	Base Metric Profile	DMTF		a metric provided directly without a dependency on other metric values
direct metric	IEEE 1061	IEEE Standard for a Software Quality Metrics Methodology	IEEE	software engineering	a metric that does not depend upon a measure of any other attribute
interval metric	DSP1053_1.0.1	Base Metric Profile	DMTF		metric that apply to a time interval. An example of an interval metric is the average CPU utilization of a server over the past hour
metric	GFD-R-P.098	Usage Record - Format Recommendation	OGF	web service	This attribute identifies the method of measurement used for quantifying the associated resource consumption if there are multiple methods by which to measure resource usage
metric	IEEE Std 610.12-1990	IEEE Standard Glossary of Software Engineering Terminology	IEEE	software engineering	a quantitative measure of the degree to which a system, component, or process possesses a given variable
metric	NIST SP 500-209	Software Error Analysis	NIST	software engineering	The definition, algorithm or mathematical function used to make a quantitative assessment of product or process.
metric	www.prosci.com/metrics.htm	-	-	business	A metric is nothing more than a standard measure to assess your performance in a particular area.

Term	Source	Title	Organization	Category	Description
metric	IEEE 1061	IEEE Standard for a Software Quality Metrics Methodology	IEEE	software engineering	see software quality metric
metric	SAMATE	SAMATE Project	NIST	software assurance	we use metric for more abstract, higher-level, or somewhat subjective attributes
metric	GB917 rev3	SLA Handbook	TMForum		a commonly identified and measurable concept
metric	ITIL 2011 glossary	glossary and abbreviations	ITIL	IT service management	Something that is measured and reported to help manage a process, IT service or activity.
metric	Merriam-Webster Dictionary		Merriam-Webster Dictionary		
software metric	Wikipedia	Software Metric	Wikipedia	software	a software is a measure of some property of a piece of software or its specifications
software quality metric	IEEE 1061	IEEE Standard for a Software Quality Metrics Methodology	IEEE	software engineering	a function whose inputs are software data and whose output is a single numerical value that can be interpreted as the degree to whichsoftware possesses a given attribute that affects its quality
summation metric	DSP1053_1.0.1	Base Metric Profile	DMTF		a type of counter metric that reflects the accumulation of a value
watermark metric	DSP1053_1.0.1	Base Metric Profile	DMTF		a type of aggregation metric used to capture the minimum or maximum value recorder for a monitored value

key performance indicator

Term	Source	Title	Organization	Category	Description
key performance indicator	ITIL 2011 glossary	glossary and abbreviations	ITIL	IT service management	A metric that is used to help manage an IT service, process, plan, project or other activity. Key performance indicators are used to measure the achievement of critical success factors. Many metrics may be measured, but only the most important of these are defined as key performance indicators and used to actively manage and report on the process, IT service or activity. They should be selected to ensure that efficiency, effectiveness and cost effectiveness are all managed.
key performance indicator	GB917 rev3	SLA Handbook	TMForum		in a telecom concept, metric close to telecom technologies and devices

benchmark

Term	Source	Title	Organization	Category	Description
benchmark	Oxford Dictionaries		Oxford Dictionaries		a standard or point of reference against which things may be compared or assessed
benchmark	Wikipedia		Wikipedia	computer	the act of running a computer program, a set of programs, or other operations, in order to assess the relative performance of an object, normally by running a number of standard tests and trials against it
benchmarking	Oxford Dictionaries		Oxford Dictionaries		evaluate or check (something) by comparison with a standard
benchmarking	Wikipedia		Wikipedia	business	the process of comparing one's business processes and performance metrics to industry bests or best practices from other industries

measurement

Term	Source	Title	Organization	Category	Description
estimator	GB917 rev3	SLA Handbook	TMForum		method to obtain or compute a measured value of a metric (alsothe value itself)
measurement	Journal of research NBS Vol. 86, No 3, May-June 1981	Foundation of Metrology	NBS	metrology	A measurement is a series of manipulations of physical objects or systems according to a defined protocol which results in a number. The number is proported to uniquely represent the magnitude (or intensity) of some quantity embodied in the test object. This number is acquired to form the basis of a decision effecting some human goal or satisfying some human need to satisfaction of which depends on the properties of test object
measurement	JCGM 200:2012	International vocabulary of metrology - Basic and general concepts and associated terms	BIPM	metrology	process of experimentaly obtaining onr or more quantity values that can reasonably be attributed to a quantity
measurement	ISO/IEC 15939	Systems and Software Engineering - Measurement Process	ISO/IEC	software engineering	Set of operations having the object of determining a value of a measure
measurement	SMM	Structured Metrics Metamodel (SMM)	OMG	software engineering	a numerical or symbolic value assigned to an entity by a measure

measurement unit

Term	Source	Title	Organization	Category	Description
unit of measure	SMM	Structured Metrics Metamodel (SMM)	OMG	software engineering	a quantity in terms of which the magnitudes of other quantities within the same total order can be stated
measurement unit	JCGM 200:2012	International vocabulary of metrology - Basic and general concepts and associated terms	BIPM	metrology	real scalar quantity, defined and adopted by convention, with which any other quantity of the same kind can be compared to express the ratio of the two quantities as a number

34

Annex C - References

1. Gray, M., "Applicability of Metrology to Information Technology," *J. Res. Natl. Stand. Technol.*, Vol. 104,No. 6, pp. 567-578, 1999.

2. Mell, P., Grance, T., "The NIST Definition of Cloud Computing," *NIST Special Publication 800-145*, 2011.

3. ISO/IEC 20926:2009, Software and systems engineering - Software measurement - IFPUG functional size measurement method.

4. ISO/IEC 19761:2011, Software engineering - COSMIC: A functional size measurement method.

5. ISO/IEC 29881:2010, Information technology - Software and systems engineering - FiSMA 1.1 functional size measurement method.

6. ISO/IEC 15939:2007, Systems and software engineering - Measurement Process.

7. JCGM 200:2012, International vocabulary of metrology - Basic and general concepts and associated terms (VIM) 3rd edition, 2012.

8. Siegel, J., Perdue, J., "Cloud Services Measures for Global Use: The Service Measurement Index (SMI)," *Service Research & Innovation Institute (SRII) Global Conference*, Published by IEEE, San Jose, CA, July 24-27, 2012.

9. NIST Cloud Computing Reference Architecture Contract and SLA (Draft), http://collaborate.nist.gov/twiki-cloud-computing/pub/CloudComputing/RATax_Jan20_2012/NIST_CC_WG_ContractSLA_Deliverable_Draft_v1_7.pdf.

10. CSCC, Practical Guide to Service Level Agreements Version 1.0, http://www.cloudstandardscustomercouncil.org/2012_Practical_Guide_to_Cloud_SLAs.pdf.

11. DMTF DSP0263, Cloud infrastructure Management Interface (CIMI) Model and RESTful HTTP-based Protocol, 2012.

12. Mach, R., et al., "Usage Record - Format Recommendation," *GFD. 98*, 2006.

13. Unified Modeling Language version 2.0, http://www.omg.org/spec/UML/2.0/. Last accessed, November 2, 2012.

14. Stevens, S., "On the Theory of Scales of Measurement," *Science*, Vol. 103, No. 2684, pp. 677-680, 1946.